ASIAPAC CULTURE

Origins of
CHINESE
CULTURE

Compiled by Li Xiaoxiang   Illustrated by Fu Chunjiang
Translated by Y N Han

⚏ ASIAPAC ● SINGAPORE

Publisher
ASIAPAC BOOKS PTE LTD
996 Bendemeer Road #06-09
Singapore 339944
Tel: (65) 6392 8455
Fax: (65) 6392 6455
Email: asiapacbooks@pacific.net.sg

Come visit us at our Internet home page
www.asiapacbooks.com

First published December 2001 as
Origins of Chinese Music and Art
ISBN 981-229-243-8

This revised edition
First published May 2005
3rd edition January 2008

© 2001 ASIAPAC BOOKS, SINGAPORE
ISBN 13   978-981-229-407-4
ISBN 10   981-229-407-4

Cover illustrations by Fu Chunjiang
Cover design by Chin Boon Leng and Kelly Lim
Body text in 11pt Times New Roman
Printed in Singapore by Chung Printing

Publisher's Note

Origins of Chinese Culture has been divided into three distinct sections:
- Section 1 explores the origins of the Chinese language and the evolution of Chinese characters;
- Section 2 introduces the reader to the Four Treasures of the Study (brush, ink, paper and inkstone) and other stationery items; and
- Section 3 takes a look at the leisurely and artistic pursuits of the Chinese, including music, chess, calligraphy, painting, Chinese New Year painting and spring couplet.

Each chapter includes a legend that is related to the topic. Be enthralled by the many delightful tales — like how Cangjie's invention of Chinese symbols was inspired by animal footprints, and how Meng Tian used goat hair to make a superb brush.

We would like to take this opportunity to thank Fu Chunjiang for his illustrations, Li Xiaoxiang for her compilation, and Y N Han for her translation. Our appreciation, too, to the production team for their best efforts in putting this book together.

Chinese Culture Series (illustrated)
Origins of Chinese Music
Origins of Chinese Names
Origins of Chinese People and Customs
Origins of Chinese Festivals
Origins of Chinese Culture
Origins of Chinese Folk Arts
Origins of Chinese Martial Arts
Origins of Chinese Cuisine
Origins of Chinese Food Culture
Origins of Chinese Tea and Wine
Origins of Chinese Science & Technology
Origins of Shaolin Kung Fu

Preface to the Chinese Culture Series

Tens of thousands of years ago, the eastern part of the northern hemisphere was a wide expanse of land which was populated by a group of people. They learnt to gather wood and make fires. They started to hunt, fish and farm. They invented written text. They created culture. They established a nation.

They were the earliest Huaxia people who prospered and multiplied to become the largest ethnic group on Earth. They developed by leaps and bounds to forge a dazzling culture. Many a brilliant ancient civilisation has been swallowed up by the currents of time, but the Huaxia culture has managed to survive. In fact, it continues to exert its influence today, not only within China, but also without, via the Silk Road, migration, etc.

The flames of wars erupted. Dynasties rose and fell. Despite the changing faces of political power, the essence of the Chinese people has remained unchanged.

Today, the Chinese people are not merely an ethnic group, but a larger cultural entity spread all over the world.

The most distinguishing aspect of Chinese culture is its all-encompassing nature. It emphasises justice and moral integrity, human relations, the power of music and rituals to cultivate the hearts of men, and the oneness of Man and Heaven... all at the same time. Next is its wisdom — it engineers invention and change, and is prolific and dynamic. Last but not least is its ingenuity — it is ever progressive and enlightening.

Taking a flying leap into the global lake of the world, the ancient Chinese culture exudes the vitality of youth!

Li Xiaoxiang
11 November 2001

About the Compiler

Li Xiaoxiang 李小香 was born in 1946. After graduating from Hu'nan Normal University in 1969, she taught Chinese language and literature in a high school. Later, she worked in Zhejiang University as a staff member of the Higher Education Research Department, an Office Administrator in the Economics Department, and as editor of an academic journal.

Besides having a firm foundation in Chinese language and literature, Li is also skilled in editorial work. She has a deep understanding of traditional Chinese culture, especially Buddhism, and has penned several discourses on this subject.

With her penchant for writing, she has produced 20-odd literary pieces and works on various topics. Her published works for the children's market include *The Story of Xinqiji, The Story of a Junior Barber, The Story of a Fisherman and a Goldfish*, and *Wisdom in Chinese Proverbs*.

She is presently a Senior Editor with Wuhan University Press.

About the Illustrator

Fu Chunjiang, born in 1974, is a native of Chongqing municipality in southeastern China. A lover of traditional Chinese culture, he graduated in Chinese language studies.

He has been fond of drawing from childhood, and since 1994, he has been drawing comics. Among his works are *The Story of Kites* and *The Faint-Hearted Hero,* as well as the bestsellers *Origins of Chinese Festivals* and *Origins of Chinese People & Customs* published by Asiapac Books. He also participated in the production of *One Riddle for One Story.*

Contents

THE CHINESE LANGUAGE

Chinese characters are one of the most ancient forms of writing whereby the form, pronunciation and meaning are all expressed. There are approximately 60,000 Chinese characters in all but only about 3,000 are commonly used.

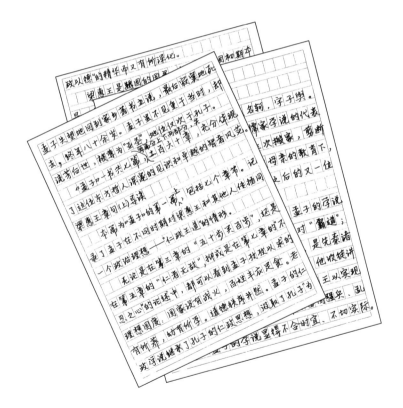

• **Chinese Characters**   • **Character Riddles**

CHAPTER *1*

CHINESE
CHARACTERS

Before writing was invented, the Chinese used knotted ropes and inscriptions on wood as memory aids.

Chinese characters originated from drawings. The earliest Chinese writing was the shell-and-bone style during the Shang Dynasty. Shell-and-bone is a type of pictography. As there was no paper during that time, inscriptions were made on tortoise shells and animal bones, hence the term shell-and-bone style.

Knotted ropes and inscriptions on wood

Animal shells and bones have other uses too.

Shell-and-bone style

3

How Chinese Characters Were Formed

The first Chinese characters were modelled after the shape of objects.

 日 (sun)　　 月 (moon)　　 山 (mountain)　　 水 (water)

As the number of words represented by drawing is limited, other methods of forming words were created.

Self-explanatory characters

Punctuation marks are used to convey the meaning of a character.

Example: A dot is added to the character *dao* 刀 (knife) to form *ren* 刃 (edge of a knife), highlighting the sharpest point of the knife.

Associative compounds

These are formed from two or more elements. The new character conveys a new meaning.

Example: *Xiu* 休 (rest) is formed from *ren* 人 (man) and *mu* 木 (wood), where the two characters combine to form a new character. It depicts a man leaning against a tree.

The shape-and-sound-based

Here, a radical that represents the meaning and another that represents the sound of the character are combined. Ninety percent of Chinese characters belong to this category.

Example: During the ancient times, there was a musical instrument called *yu* that was made of *zhu* 竹 (bamboo). Hence, *zhu* is used as a radical while the sound element is represented by the element *yu* 于. Hence the character *yu* 竽 is formed.

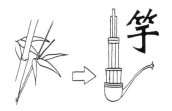

The Evolution of Chinese Characters

Shell-and-bone style	Bronze inscriptions	Small-seal style	Official style	Regular style
魚	魚	魚	魚	魚
鹿	鹿	鹿	鹿	鹿
鳥	鳥	鳥	鳥	鳥

The shell-and-bone style of Chinese writing goes a long way back. Over time, the strokes evolved from drawings to writing, from pictographs to symbols and from complicated to simple. Following the shell-and-bone style, writings inscribed on bronzeware were also practised during the Shang and Western Zhou Dynasties.

When Emperor Qin unified China, he also had writing styles unified in the form of *xiaozhuan* 小篆 (small-seal style). Later, the emperor further simplified *xiaozhuan* to form *lishu* 隶书 (official style). This style broke new ground as it broke away from pictographs. Towards the end of the Han Dynasty, *kaishu* 楷书 (regular style) was developed with *lishu* as its foundation. The advent of *kaishu* structured Chinese writing and gave it the firm and solid structure that we see today.

Some Interesting Chinese Characters

Ren (man)

The character *ren* looks like a man turning to his left. His head and body are slightly bent forward while his hands are outstretched. He looks like he is busy with something. Initially, his head and his limbs were drawn in detail. Later, his limbs were simplified and so was his head. Next, his neck and limbs were joined by two falling strokes to form the character *ren* as we know it today.

Two persons leaning against each other = *bei* (back)

Two persons fighting each other = *dou* (fight)

Two persons standing in line = *bi* (compare)

One person following another = *cong* (follow)

Shou (hand)

The character *shou* looks like a man's palm. There are five fingers in all, with the middle one being the longest. To make writing easier, the fingers were drawn as lines. Finally, when it evolved into one stroke and two horizontal lines, we could see the fingers no more.

The hand clawing downwards to grab something = *zhua* (grab)

The hand picking something = *cai* (pick)

Two hands fighting for the same thing = *zheng* (fight)

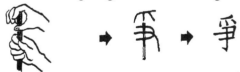

Using the hand to support someone = *fu* (support)

Kou (mouth)

The character *kou* is like an open mouth. In the beginning, it was semi-circular in shape. It later became a square.

Four teeth inside a mouth = *chi* (teeth)

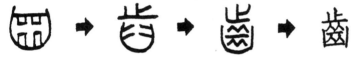

Tongue sticking out of a mouth = *she* (tongue)

Delicious food inside a mouth = *gan* (sweet)

Many mouths transmit wisdom over generations = *gu* (ancient)

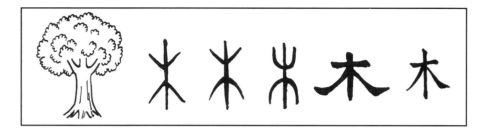

Mu (tree)

The character *mu* is similar to a tree, which has its branches at the top, its trunk in the middle and its roots at the bottom. The tree trunk is represented by a vertical line, the tree branches by a horizontal line and its roots, two falling strokes.

Two trees together symbolise many trees = *lin* (woods)

Three trees together mean more trees = *sen* (forest)

The roots of a tree are at the bottom = *ben* (origin)

A tree bearing fruit = *guo* (fruit)

The Chinese People's Attitude Towards Chinese Characters

Reverence for writing

The ancient people held Chinese writings in reverence. They believed that Chinese writings were a holy creation of the saints and must not be treated in a slipshod manner. In various parts of China, one will find special urns built to burn pieces of paper with writings on them, reflecting the ancient people's deep reverence for writing.

Talisman

They also believed that the writings could protect and bless them. Thus, the talisman, a piece of paper with writing on it, was created. It was believed to possess mysterious spiritual power and could protect one from evil forces.

Auspicious writing

Today, Chinese like to put up words like *fu* 福 (happiness), *chun* 春 (spring) and *man* 满 (fullness) to embellish pictures and sculptures or to be pasted on buildings, ornaments and even clothing. It expresses the people's wish for a happy and prosperous life.

Cangjie Invents Chinese Characters

Legend has it that the Yellow Emperor's official recorder Cangjie is the man behind the first Chinese characters. Cangjie was in charge of livestock and rations.

The livestock and rations keep increasing. Keeping track of them is tough.

I must think of a way to help me keep track of them.

By using ropes of different colours, I'll be able to distinguish the different types of livestock and rations.

The number of knots on the ropes will indicate the quantity.

This is not good. If the quantity decreases and there is no way I can undo the knots, then…

Got it! I'll use shells instead. When the quantity rises, I'll add more shells; when it drops, I'll remove some shells. That's simple and convenient!

Seeing how capable Cangjie was, the Yellow Emperor entrusted him with more responsibilities.

You shall also keep a record of the number of times we pray to the gods, the allocation of hunters and the population census.

Just using more ropes and more shells won't be enough now…

Cangjie happened to be on a hunting trip one day.

Head east and we'll find antelopes.

No, if we head north, we'll find deer.

No! Two tigers have just gone westward. It'll be a pity if we give them a miss.

Elders, how did you know where the different creatures can be found?

Do you see the different animal footprints on the ground?

Oh... A different footprint represents a particular creature. Why can't I use different symbols to represent the different things I have to oversee?

What symbol shall I use for the cattle? It has to be something easy to remember.

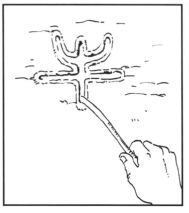

Right, I'll use this symbol!

Next will be the birds, the goats, the fishes…

By using diffferent symbols, Cangjie's work was made much easier.

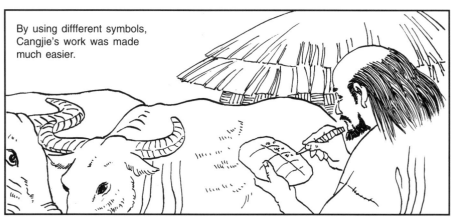

Cangjie, the symbols you drew are very useful.

Teach them to the others.

Yes.

The usage of these symbols became common over time. People began to use these symbols as a tool of communication. They paved the way for the formation of Chinese characters.

CHAPTER *2*

CHARACTER RIDDLES

The history of Chinese character riddles goes a long way back. It has been around for more than 3,500 years.

Cryptic language

Riddles are made up of cryptic language where metaphors and symbolisms are used. One example would be King Jie of the Xia Dynasty who compared himself to the sun in the sky. He said, "Just as I have the land under Heaven, so has the sun the sky. If the sun perishes, I perish."

The people hated the tyrannical King Jie. They vented their frustration through the cryptic saying: "If the tyrannical sun perishes, everything else shall perish along with it." King Jie was compared to the tyrannical sun. So long as the tyrannical sun would perish, the people were willing to perish along with it.

Just as I have the land under Heaven, so has the sun the sky.

Character riddle

Character riddles are a type of Chinese riddles. They make use of the interchangeability of the meaning, pronunciation and form of Chinese characters.

Example:
二形一体，四支八头，一八五八，飞泉仰流。
Er xing yi ti, si zhi ba tou, yi ba wu ba, fei quan yang liu.
The answer to the riddle is *jing* 井 (well).

The first line says two *er* form one entity; the second line says there are four pillars (*si zhi*) and eight heads (*ba tou*); in the third line, *yi ba* refers to the eight corners of a well while *wu ba* means four tens, ie. four of the character *shi* (ten). Every line gives us the character *jing* (well).

So the answer to the riddle is *jing*. It's certainly a tough one!

Lantern riddle

Ancient China celebrated *yuanxiao* 元宵 (the 15th day of the first lunar month) by holding a lantern festival. Riddles would be pasted on these lanterns and everyone could take a stab at them. These riddles became known as lantern riddles over time.

Prediction through character

It was also common among the people to predict one's fortune by breaking up a character. For example, if the character *you* is used to predict the fortunes of a nation, it will be most inauspicious. The character *you* is the character *fan* (to rebel) with its head sticking out. It means that rebels have made their appearance.

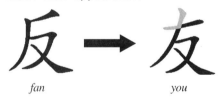

fan   *you*

Object riddle

Besides character riddles, Chinese riddles also include object riddles. These riddles smack of everyday life and their solutions are concrete objects.

Example: A small long-legged creature likes flying into bridal chambers and loves flower wine. When you clap your hands, it dies. The answer is mosquito.

The Premier Writes

During the 13th year of Jian'an (AD 208), Emperor Hanxian made Cao Cao the premier and had an opulent and luxurious residence built for the latter.

One day, Cao Cao's counsellor, Yang Xiu, was showing him around the new residence.

Premier, that's the back garden.

Hmm... Go get me a brush.

Yang Xiu

Your Excellency, why did the premier write the character *huo* on the door?

When you have *huo* within a *men* (door), it forms the character *kuo*.

The premier is saying that the door to the garden is too small. He wants it expanded (*kuo*).

Thank you for enlightening me, Your Excellency.

When Cao Cao next visited the garden…

The door has expanded. They did understand what I was trying to tell them.

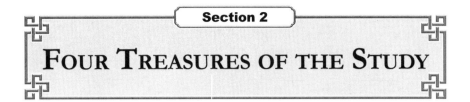

FOUR TREASURES OF THE STUDY

In ancient times, brushes, ink, paper and seals were indispensable in writing and painting. Together, they were termed the "Four Treasures of the Study".

• **Brush**   • **Ink**   • **Paper**   • **Inkstone**   • **Seal**

CHAPTER 3

BRUSH

The brush is a writing instrument that is peculiar to China. It is used in both calligraphy and painting. It was introduced into Japan during the Tang Dynasty. Today, it can be found all over the world.

The brush comprises the hair tip and the stick. The hair tip is made from the hairs of the hare, goat, horse, mouse, wolf, fox, gorilla, swan, duck, chicken, pig, baby or even the human beard.

The brush stick may be made of various types of bamboo, ivory, horn, jade, crystal, coloured glaze, gold, silver or porcelain.

Let's look at some interesting brushes below.

Qinghua yunlong brush 青花云龙管鬃毫提笔

It was produced during the Qing Dynasty. The brush stick is made from porcelain while the tip is made from pig hair. This facilitates a strong writing style.

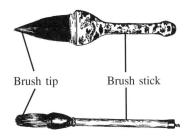

Brush tip   Brush stick

Changfeng yanghao brush 长锋羊毫笔

This was produced during the Qing Dynasty. The hair tip is made from goat hair. This brush is very durable.

Langhao painting brush 狼毫书画笔

This is a common type of brush and is made from weasel hair. It was often used for drawing and writing in *xiaokai*.

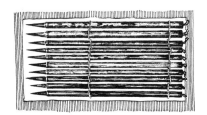

The Development of the Brush

Brushes were already in existence more than 2,000 years ago. Though there was no concrete evidence to prove the existence of brushes during the Western Zhou Dynasty, inscriptions on painted pottery and shell-and-bone writings indicated the use of brushes.

Inscriptions on painted pottery

Shell-and-bone writing

During the Eastern Zhou Dynasty, it was common to write on bamboo slats using brushes. If an error was made on the bamboo slat, a knife would be used to carve away the wrong character. Hence, besides the use of a brush, one must also have a small knife at hand while writing.

Carving away a wrong character with a small knife

Early brushes either had the brush tips wrapped round the stick with a silk thread or the hair clamped inside a split bamboo stick. During the Qin Dynasty, General Meng Tian improved on the brush. Its making was very close to what we have today.

The early brush

The improved brush

25

An Alternative Use for the Brush

During the Qin-Han times, people (especially court officials) liked to wear a brand new brush on their heads as an ornament. It was known as the *zanbai* brush 簪白笔. Brushes then measured about 20 cm long. Come the Wei-Jin times, the *zanbai* brush, which was getting shorter and shorter, was no longer popular.

Famous Brushes

Xuan brush 宣笔

This renowned brush from the Tang Dynasty was made from hare fur. The tip of the brush is very pointed. It was used as an article of tribute to the court in those days.

Various types of *xuan* brush

Hu brush 湖笔

Shanlian of Huzhou in Zhejiang enjoys a reputation as the capital of brushes. Almost every household knows how to make a brush. The hair tip of the *hu* brush was made from goat hair. The hair has to be soaked, plucked, combined and brushed. There are more than 70 steps involved in the making of *hu* brush. This strict adherence to the steps involved ensures that the three rules of excellence, purity and beauty and four virtues of sharpness, neatness, roundness and strength are maintained.

The world-renowned *hu* brush

Decorated Brushes

The cleverness of the ancient craftsmen enabled them to inscribe drawings and scenery on the brush stick. The brush was not just a functional tool but also became a collectible kept as a work of art.

The Story of the *Hu* Brush

The *hu* brush is the most famous among all the brushes in China. It is made in Shanlian Town, 70 km from the south part of Huzhou, Zhejiang Province. Behind the *hu* brush is a beautiful story…

In order to build a new palace and the Great Wall of China, Qin Shihuang had the people's assets seized. He also sent General Meng Tian to deliver soldiers' wages.

Help! Someone has jumped into the river!

Who are you? Why did you jump into the river?

My name is Pu Xianglian. My father has been taken away to build the Great Wall and my mother has just passed away...

The emperor and his ambitious endeavours have caused the people much misery and broken up many families!

We had no more rice at home and the officials were forcing us to hand over our rations and money. I was at my wits' end, so I decided to jump into the river...

Take this money.

Meng Tian chose to stay in Shanlian Town where goats were in abundance.

My mother's death anniversary is in two days' time. I'd like you to help me pen an elegiac address.

No problem. I will need a brush.

I have a white cloth and some ash.

But there is no brush.

One year later...

Xianglian, are you in?

Give me a bamboo stick and some goat hair.

If I fix the goat hair on the end of a bamboo stick, I'll have a brush!

30

The next day...

In the past, I wrote with deer hair.

This is my first try at writing with goat hair. I'm not used to it.

Isn't this the brush General Meng Tian used yesterday?

Why did he throw it into the lime crock?

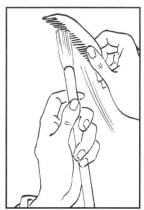

31

One day, Meng Tian went to visit Xianglian again.

Where did you get such a lovely brush?

This was the brush you left behind the other time.

It had dropped into the lime crock. I washed it and brushed the hair. That removed the blunt hairs.

Let me try writing with it.

It's a good brush! It writes well!

After being soaked in lime, the oil on the goat hair was removed. That makes writing with it so much easier.

From now on, I plan to make brushes with this method. Would you help me?

Yes, I would.

The two of them later got married and made brushes for a living. As the two of them first met in a lake *(hu)*, they called their brushes *(bi) hubi*.

After the news of Pu Xianglian helping Meng Tian make brushes spread, their fellow villagers approached them for advice on making brushes.

After the death of Meng Tian and Pu Xianglian, the villagers built an ancestral hall in memory of them.

Inside the hall were the statues of Meng Tian and Pu Xianglian. Later, the people paid homage to Meng Tian as the Forefather of Brushes and Pu Xianglian, the Goddess of Brushes.

CHAPTER *4*

INK

Where there is brush, there is ink. Before ink was invented, Man used carving to inscribe words.

The people of the Shang Dynasty were already using ink. Characters were written on tortoise shells which were later placed over a flame. The ancient people used the lines shown on the heated shells to predict their fortunes.

Telling one's fortune from the tortoise shell

The Earliest Ink

From the Qin to Han Dynasties, ink was made from natural lime like coal. The ink was known as black lead. During the Three Kingdoms Period, ink was made by burning pinewood or lacquer. The soot remains were made into ink powder. During the Tang Dynasty, ink was made from the burning of tung oil and lacquer.

Burning pinewood to make ink from its soot

The Invention of Ink

Rubber was blended into ink during the Jin Dynasty to form ink balls. This type of ink was very glossy. Rubbing the ink stick on the inkstone formed ink.

During ancient imperial examinations, candidates had to spend time rubbing the ink stick on the inkstone. It was a time-consuming activity and it did not help that the ink dried very fast. It was not until the late Qing Dynasty that someone's ingenuity saw the creation of bottled liquid ink.

← Liquid ink

The Treasure of All Inks

Jijin ink 集锦墨 was highly popular during the Ming and Qing Dynasties. *Jijin* ink refers to the various types of famous ink sticks that are contained in an exquisite box. Scenery, personalities, flora and fauna, fish, insects and poems were etched on these ink sticks. The intricate inscription drew admiration all round.

The box used to hold these ink sticks was also an art in itself. Dragons, scenery or characters were added to the box.

The best of Chinese painting, calligraphy, carving and ink manufacture thus came together in this box of exquisite ink sticks. There, *jijin* ink became a popular choice of gift as well as a collector's item. The humble functional ink had become a work of art.

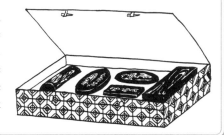

Frozen Ink

Ink dries easily in winter as it is freezing cold. Hence, in olden days, students need not practise writing in winter. Instead, they read. When spring arrived, they would pick up their brushes again.

Inventor of the Ink Stick

Legend has it that the first piece of ink stick was made by a man called Xing Yi during the Zhou Dynasty.

Xing Yi was washing his hands in the river one day when he saw a piece of floating charred pine. As he picked it up, his hand was stained black.

He took the pine charcoal home and pounded it into ash.

He then added gruel to the ash.

Finally, he kneaded the mixture into sticks. That saw the beginning of man-made ink.

The Story of *Hui* Ink

Xi Tinggui of the Tang Dynasty invented the renowned *hui* ink 徽墨. Li Tinggui's real surname was Xi. His father, Xi Chao, was an ink artisan. Father and son lived in Yishui, Hebei.

Circumstances later forced them to uproot and travel down south to make a living.

Look, this place has no lack of wood. All the materials we need to make ink can be found here.

We'll settle down here then.

Xi Tinggui and his father settled down in their new adopted home and sold ink for a living.

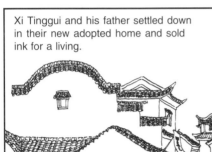

Look, I wrote this calligraphy using the ink made by the Xis.

Their ink is dark and glossy. It sits very well on paper.

Everyone in Xin'an City uses their ink.

Xi Tinggui learnt how to make ink from his father. He soon picked up the craft and mastered the art of making ink. The ink he made became more popular than that of his father's.

Mr Xi, you'll henceforth improve on the traditional method of making ink. Make me the best ink.

The ruler of Southern Tang enjoyed calligraphy and painting. One day, he summoned Xi Tinggui.

Yes, Your Majesty.

After many trials and errors, Xi Tinggui discovered that tung soot and lacquer soot made the best ink, far surpassing pine soot.

He added gold foil to the ink. That gave the ink a sheen and lasting colour.

He even added expensive scents to the ink, thereby giving the ink a lovely scent and protecting it from insects.

He also got well-known carving artisans to inscribe on the ink sticks, thereby creating exquisite works of art.

This is the latest ink stick.

Let us all admire it together.

What a lovely scent!

Rubbing the ink stick will no longer be such a chore.

This ink is dark and glossy. It's fantastic!

It's truly a gem!

Emperor Li later made Xi Tinggui an ink official and bestowed on him the surname Li. The ink Xi Tinggui created is *hui* ink, also known as Tinggui ink.

CHAPTER 5

PAPER

One of China's four great inventions was paper — an invention which contributed to the spread of culture in no small way.

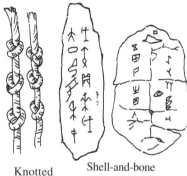

Before paper was invented, knotted ropes and inscriptions on animal shells and bones and bronzeware were the earliest forms of note-taking.

Knotted ropes

Shell-and-bone inscription

It was much later that Man began to write on bamboo slips, wooden slats or cloth and to carve characters on stones.

Inscription on bronzeware

41

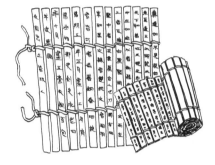

Before paper was invented, characters were written on thin bamboo or wooden slats that were joined to form a scroll.

The Invention of Paper

The earliest type of paper was made of silk wadding. To make winter clothing, the ancient people would cook silkworm cocoons in water. After that, the cocoons were soaked and tumbled in water. That turned the cocoons into silk wadding for the making of cloth. The silk wadding would leave a thin layer of cloth fibre on the bamboo mat and that became a writing material.

During the Eastern Han Dynasty, a clever official by the name of Cai Lun improved on the production of paper. He mixed tree bark, flax, cloth fragments and fish net together. The end result was a paper that had minimal impurities. The paper was white and made for easier writing.

Cai Lun making paper

Famous Paper

As the method of making paper kept improving, that gave rise to a wide variety of paper and also produced top-grade paper.

Xuan paper 宣纸	This was already seen before the Tang Dynasty. It is soft, firm and white, and is especially good for painting and calligraphy. Given its ideal texture, it brings out the intended meaning of the painting and calligraphy. It is also resistant to ageing and worms. The *xuan* paper is also hailed as "the king of all papers".
Xuetao paper 薛涛笺	The poetess Xue Tao of the Tang Dynasty was the creator of the *xuetao* paper. Juice from the cottonrose hibiscus was added to the ingredients used in making paper. The clean, exquisite paper is deep red and is used to pen poems.
Xiegong paper 谢公笺	Xie Jingchu of the Song Dynasty created this paper of 10 colours for the purpose of sending messages. There is deep red, pink, yellow, bright yellow, dark blue, light blue, dark green, light green, copper green and pale white. It enjoyed the same popularity as the *xuetao* paper.
Chengxintang paper 澄心堂纸	This *xuan* paper was produced in Huizhou during the Tang Dynasty. It is seen as the cream of the crop. It is white and pristine. As Emperor Li of the Tang Dynasty favoured this paper, it was kept in Chengxin Hall. As such, the paper became known as *chengxintang* paper.
Shuiwen paper 水纹纸	This was a well-known paper from the Tang Dynasty. If placed against the light, one can see the fine lines and graphics on it.
Jinsu paper 金粟笺纸	This was used for writing and printing sutras. It is hard and solid. Besides being very durable, it is both water-resistant and worm-resistant.

All these papers are very valuable. Do use them appropriately.

The Spread of Paper

In AD 105, Cai Lun contributed greatly to human civilisation by making improvements to the method of paper production. Subsequently, the Chinese method of paper-making spread to the following places:

- Korea and Vietnam in the fourth century
- Japan and the Arabian countries in the seventh century
- Egypt in the 10th century
- Morocco in the 11th century
- Europe and Africa during the 12th to 16th centuries
- The American continent in the 17th century

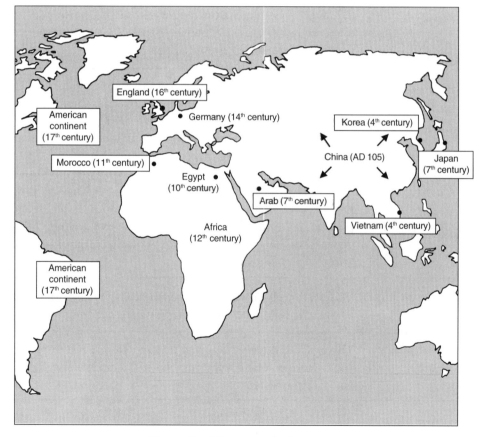

The route of the spread of paper

How Do We Preserve Paper?

Chinese painting and calligraphy are produced on paper. If we do not preserve them well, they will be easily damaged.

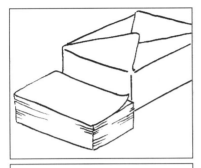

To prevent humidity and mildew: Stack the papers and wrap them up inside waxed paper. Place the parcel in a dry and well-ventilated place.

To prevent folds: Roll up the paper or store it flat. Do not fold it.

To keep it from turning yellow: Keep the paper away from direct sunlight.

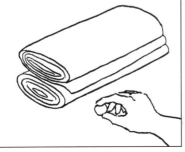

To prevent insect attacks: Smear the juice from *huangbo* 黃檗, a Chinese herb, on the paper, or place a strong-smelling agent with the paper. Alternatively, wrap the calligraphy or painting with newspaper.

The Legend of *Xuan* Paper

The *xuan* paper from Anhui is a very famous paper. It is age-resistant and worm-resistant. It was invented by Kong Dan, Cai Lun's disciple.

Upon the death of Cai Lun, Kong Dan hung up a painting of his beloved teacher. It was done on the paper he had created in memory of the former.

Why did the paper turn yellow and black? It's even torn...

A year later...

In order to create a paper that would not turn yellow, Kong Dan decided to conduct a study at the various paper mills all over the country.

After travelling for more than 10 years, Kong Dan, who was already in his 30s, still could not find the method to making good paper.
One day, he arrived in Xuancheng, Jiangnan.

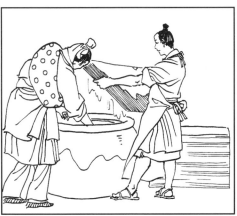

This white stuff resembles paper.

It's as soft as cotton but as tough as rubber. It will be great for making paper!

Madam, what's the white thing on that big tree?

After lying in the river for so long, the tree bark from this wingceltis has dropped off from the trunk.

The white thing you saw is the loose tree bark.

That's called a wingceltis (*tan*檀). It fell into the river the year my granddaughter was born.

My granddaughter was hence called Tangu.

This is wonderful!

Kong Dan thus settled down by the river.

Tangu, I must invent the best paper there is.

Brother Kong, let me help you.

Together, they worked hard at making paper.

Tangu, would you marry me?

Yes, but only after you have created the best paper in the world.

After countless tests, Kong Dan finally succeeded in making a top-grade paper.

Brother Kong, congratulations!

Let's give this paper a name.

It was made in Xuancheng. Let's call it *xuan* paper.

Kong Dan had the painting of his teacher redone on the paper he had made and married Tangu.

In the years that followed, people began to use *xuan* paper in their calligraphy and painting.

Some ancient paintings and calligraphy are still around today, all thanks to the lasting quality of *xuan* paper.

CHAPTER **6**

INKSTONE

In China, the inkstone is used together with brushes and ink. Early ink was made of black lead or some other minerals. Before one could paint or write, the black lead had to be pounded and water added before use. As such, a pestle accompanied the earliest inkstone.

The inkstone and the pestle

It was not until the Han Dynasty that man-made ink was invented. Ink could be used on the inkstone directly. Hence, black lead gradually made its exit.

The inkstone on its own

The Earliest Inkstone

In a mausoleum that dated back more than 5,000 years, archaeologists found an inkstone lying next to the skeleton of a primitive man. There was even a stone lid and a stone pestle in the hollow of the inkstone. There were several ink sticks and five grey ceramic cups as well. The items formed a complete ceramic set.

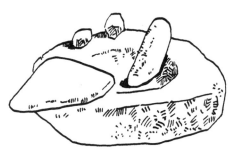

The earliest inkstone

The Development of the Inkstone

Before the Tang Dynasty, there were no tables or chairs with legs. People would sit on straw mats and write on very low tables. To accommodate such a situation, the inkstones during that time were round so that more ink could be stored. The inkstones had legs to prop them up so that they would tilt to one side, making it easier for the brush to dip into them.

Towards the end of the Tang Dynasty, tall tables and chairs made their appearance. The inkstone was thus moved onto the table. Gradually, inkstones without legs became more common.

A round inkstone with legs

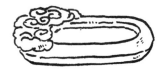

An inkstone without legs

Four Famous Inkstones

An inkstone has many forms. Not only is it a writing tool, it is also a piece of art.

Before the Tang Dynasty, inkstones were made from cobblestone, sandstone, porcelain, bronze, silver, lacquer, iron and ceramic. When it came to the Tang and Song Dynasties, materials of excellent quality like *duan* stone 端石, *xi* stone 歙石 and *taohe* stone 洮河石 were used. The *duan* inkstone, *xi* inkstone, *tao* inkstone and *dengni* inkstone became known as the Four Famous Inkstones.

***Duan* inkstone** 端 硯	*Duan* stone was formed about some 600 million years ago. It boasts of many lines and rare stone eyes. It is as smooth as jade and has an excellent quality for holding ink.
***Xi* inkstone** 歙硯	*Xi* stone was formed about one billion years ago. Black in colour, it has intricate lines. It is even and firm after years of use, and stays as good as new.
***Tao* inkstone** 洮 硯	It is found in deep waters and is not readily found. The stone is intricate and clear. Its lines are as fine as silk and it comes in green and red colours.
***Dengni* inkstone** 澄泥硯	This is made of sticky earth. The method involves 10 steps. The quality is firm and sturdy. This inkstone comes in many colours.

Mining for Inkstones

The mining work involved hundreds and thousands of workers.

The workers mined for inkstones wearing only a loincloth. With an oil-lamp and a rope to guide them, they crawled into the hole.

If water was present, the miners had to drain the water from the stone before they could begin their work.

As one miner hacked at the stone, another would lie down and hold the oil-lamp to provide light.

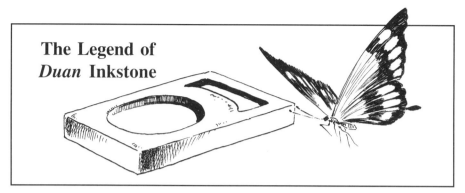

The Legend of *Duan* Inkstone

The *duan* inkstone is one of China's Four Famous Inkstones. It is said that in a little mountain village in Duanzhou, there was a poor scholar called Ah Duan.

He loved reading so much that he often forgot to cut firewood.

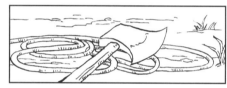

This butterfly is such a nuisance!

All right, I'll go and cut firewood.

Whoosh!

Who hung this colourful curtain here?

Where am I?

Ah! It's actually a swarm of butterflies!

This place has nothing but stones. There is no way out.

I'm so hungry.

Never mind, I'll continue with my reading.

Bookworm!

Duan.

...
...

Did you call me?

Marrying you is like having married a tree. You bury yourself in your books all day and neglect me.

...
...

I feel very lonely.

Die, I'll stop reading those wretched books from now on. I'll chat with you.

Don't be angry.

Duan kept his promise and put his books aside. But he gradually lost his appetite and looked despondent.

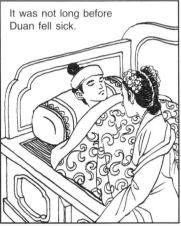

It was not long before Duan fell sick.

Not even the miracle pill can help him.

Perhaps he'll feel better if I return him his books.

Duan, look.

Ah, my book!

Seeing it revives me. Die, I'm feeling better already.

You only love your book.

Let's go our separate ways.

Strange, how come his ink doesn't freeze?

Among all the candidates, only Duan has finished his essay.

How strange.

May I try your inkstone?

Please.

The ink on your inkstone doesn't get frozen!

This inkstone is a gem. I must show it to His Majesty.

Please do.

Soon after...

His Majesty has named the inkstone "*duan* inkstone". It shall henceforth be an article of tribute.

Duan shall now be the magistrate of Duanzhou. You shall oversee the mining of stones for the *duan* inkstone.

From then on, the fame of the *duan* inkstone spread far and wide. It soon became a treasure of the study.

CHAPTER 7

SEAL AND OTHER STATIONERY ITEMS

Other than the brush, ink, paper and inkstone — the Four Treasures of the Study — there were other indispensable stationery items. But they are seldom used in modern times.

Brush stand
Used to hold brushes, this was often in the shape of mountain peaks where brushes are placed in the hollowed parts.

Brush holder
When not in use, brushes are placed in it. They were often made of porcelain, jade, bamboo and wood. They could either be cylindrical or rectangular.

Rinse dish
After every use, the brush would be rinsed in this dish. Very often, it was in the shape of a fish bowl.

Ink bed
After each rubbing, the damp ink stick would be placed on the ink bed to dry.

Paper weight
It was used to hold down papers or books to keep them flat. They usually took on the forms of animals.

Water jug
Either cylindrical or rectangular, it was used to add water to the inkstone for rubbing purposes.

Ink drip
This was used for the storage of liquid ink.

Arm guard
This was placed below the arm to prevent ink from dirtying one's arm.

Poetry slip holder
Made of bamboo, it was used to hold everyday poems.

Ink paste box
Used to keep ink paste, it was commonly made of porcelain and jade.

Ink paste was a red dye used in seals for official documents. Generally, it was made from a red pigment, moxa and oil, among other ingredients.

Seal
Often used in calligraphy and painting, the seal was usually made with special stones. In ancient times, seals were made of jade, gold, silver, iron, crystal, porcelain and ivory. Later, seals made of stone gradually took precedence, especially the precious red-stained stone.

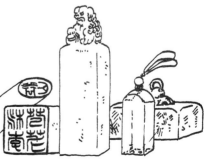

Seals can take on so many forms!

The Origins of the Seal

During the Yin and Shang Dynasties, letters and parcels were secured with a rope. To prevent unauthorised opening of mail, a piece of ink paste would be sealed on the rope. That was known as the *fengni* 封泥. Later, delivery of official documents and sealing of storehouses also used ink paste. That paved the way for the appearance of seals.

During the Zhou Dynasty, the exchange of goods increased greatly. To ensure safe transactions and storage of goods, a stamp of authenticity and trustworthiness had to be used. Therefore, seals became a heavily-used item.

Types of Seals

In ancient China, seals were classified into two broad categories — official and personal seals.

Official seals

Official seals were a symbol of power. They were ranked accordingly during ancient times. When Emperor Qin unified China, the priceless *heshibi* 和氏璧 was used to make his seal. That thus became a symbol of an emperor's authority. Whoever had possession of it would enjoy the status of an emperor.

When the emperor authorised an official to carry out a duty, it had to be accompanied by a document stamped with the seal. When an official was removed from office or transferred, he had to surrender his seal. Officials of different ranks had seals that were of varying value. These officials carried their seals with them at all times as a mark of their position and power.

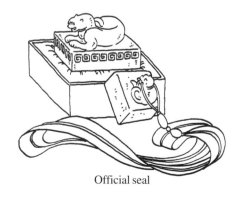

Official seal

Red-stained Stone

It is a precious stone found in Mt Yuyan in Changhua County, Zhejiang Province. It contains minerals like cinnabar and pyrophyllite. The stone gets its red colour from cinnabar while pyrophyllite comes in a variety of colours like white, yellow, grey, green and black. That gives the stone a very attractive translucent quality. The value of the red-stained stone is determined by the amount of red in it, its translucency and purity.

Red-stained stone was first discovered in the Ming Dynasty. The rich had them carved into works of art and gave them away as gifts. When it came to the Qing Dynasty, the royal family bought these stones at a high price to have them made as seals.

Personal seals

Personal seals are also known as seals. They made their appearance before official seals. They took on more interesting forms like name seals. Another type would be leisure seals, on which words of wisdom or lines from a poem were carved.

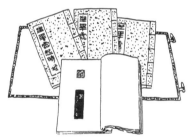

Seals were also used in one's prized collection. The ancient people loved to mark a seal on their prized collection as a show of their ownership and appreciation. Names, pet names, titles or words signifying ownership were carved on these seals.

Seals in private collections were carved with personal names, pet names or titles.

During the Qing Dynasty, a loving couple, Shen Sanbai and his wife Yunniang, had two seals made. One of them was carved with *sheng sheng shi shi* 生生世世 (for eternity) while the other, *yong wei fu fu* 永为夫妇 (husband and wife for life). Each of them possessed one seal and used it in their letters to each other.

Carving on Seals

Before the Song Dynasty, most seals served a functional purpose. They were a mark of trustworthiness. It was not until the Song and Yuan Dynasties that some officials and learned men began to appreciate seals with artistic carving. Calligraphy and painting had contributed to this trend. During the Ming Dynasty, craftsmen specialising in the carving of seals mushroomed and seals began to take on an artistic role.

Seals in Chinese Painting and Calligraphy

Seals are not only works of admiration, they are also an integral part of Chinese painting and calligraphy. Painters and calligraphers will stamp a seal bearing their names on their works. And they do not just stamp the seal once. Besides authenticating the works as theirs, the seals serve as a form of artistic expression.

The shape, style of carving, word content and position of the seal are all closely linked to the content, disposition, style and expression of the painting or calligraphy. Seals serve to add the finishing touch, balance the painting composition and add colour to the piece of work. In calligraphy, seals are often stamped near the first or the last character. However, it cannot be too near or too far from the character. In painting, the position of the seal is also important. For instance, seals are not to be stamped on the peak of a mountain or in the midst of a stream.

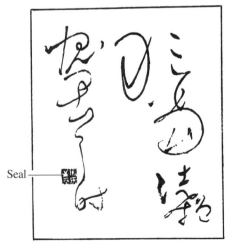

Seal ——

Seal ——

Seal ——

Seals are also an integral part of Chinese painting and calligraphy.

Su Qin and the Seals of Six States

Su Qin was a famous politician during the Warring States Period. He came from a poor family but all he did was study. Even his own family held him in contempt.

Everyone is working hard.

But your brother just reads all day. He's so useless!

That boy is hopeless.

Su Qin ignored all this talk and continued with his reading. He would poke himself with an awl whenever he was tired to keep himself awake.

Su Qin later persuaded the rulers of Yan, Zhao, Han, Wei, Qi and Chu to unite to fight against their common enemy, Qin.

With the combined forces of the six states, your power will far surpass that of Qin. That will crush Qin for sure.

The rulers of the six states made Su Qin the premier of all six states.

With seals representing the six states, Su Qin returned to his hometown. Even his sister-in-law, who used to despise him, went prostrate on the ground to welcome him without daring to look at him.

Sister-in-law, why is everyone showing me so much respect?

You are now the premier of six states. You're powerful and wealthy.

Would we still dare to treat you like we did before?

CALLIGRAPHY, PAINTING, MUSIC AND CHESS

In ancient times, calligraphy, painting, music and chess were the leisurely pursuits of the genteel set. They were also the mark of a cultured lifestyle. Not only are they an art form, they can also mould our temperament.

• Calligraphy   • Painting   • Chinese New Year Picture
• Music   • *Weiqi*   • *Xiangqi*

CHAPTER *8*

CALLIGRAPHY

Chinese calligraphy has been hailed as a type of word art, a form of emotive line dance, a soundless music and a colourless drawing. Hence, calligraphy is also called an ink dance.

The Origins of Chinese Calligraphy

Three thousand years ago, our forefathers used a combination of lines to convey the meaning behind their drawings. Carvings were also made on tortoise shells and animal bones for the same purpose. That set the precedent for the art of calligraphy.

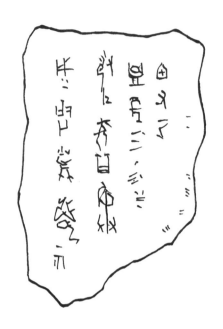

Later, through the use of the Four Treasures of the Study — brush, ink, paper and inkstone — Man began to give life and a sense of rhythm to writing by using various brush strokes and styles, compositions and presentations of ideas.

Types of Writing Styles

In calligraphy, there are various writing styles. Among them are the seal, running, regular, official and walking styles. Each style has its own unique characteristics.

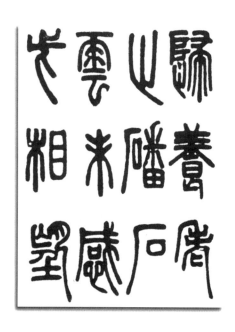

Zhuanshu 篆书 **(seal style)**
During the Qin and Han Dynasties, Chinese characters were longish and round and displayed the beauty of curved strokes.

Xingshu 行书 **(walking style)**
This is the most common style in calligraphy. It is a cross between the *kaishu* and the *caoshu*. The *Orchid Pavilion Preface* written by Wang Xizhi of the Eastern Jin Dynasty is hailed as the quintessential representative work of the *xingshu*.

Kaishu 楷书 (regular style)

A most commonly-seen style in calligraphy, the characters are squarish and regular, the strokes full and beautiful. This style reached its acme during the Tang Dynasty when the three great calligraphers of *kaishu* lived — Yan Zhenqing, Liu Gongquan and Ouyang Xun.

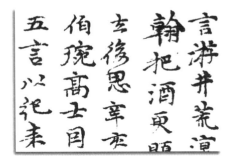

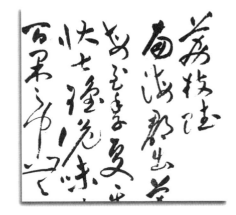

Lishu 隶书 (official style)

The characters are flat and exude the beauty of square lines.

Caoshu 草书 (running style)

It expresses the beauty of lines best with its dancing lines that are full of life and zest. It is the best style for the expression of the calligrapher's feelings and personalities. The *caoshu* creates the feel of a thunderstorm. Zhang Xu and Huai Su of the Tang Dynasty are best known for this style.

Learning Calligraphy

Learning the correct way of holding a brush is the very first step in learning calligraphy. The way we hold a brush is different from the way we hold a pen.

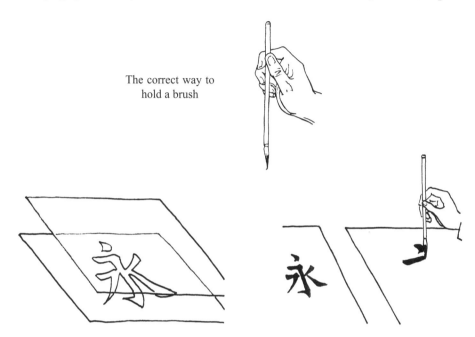

The correct way to hold a brush

Practitioners of calligraphy begin by tracing. Wielding a brush, they trace out the character that is placed below a piece of transparent paper.

After some practice, they move on to writing the character with the original piece as a reference and do away with the tracing paper all together.

Beginners of calligraphy may start with the *kaishu*. This style lays the foundation for good writing. Once you have a good grasp of it, learning the other styles is made easier.

There is no shortcut to learning calligraphy. One must keep on practising. Many famous calligraphers from China spent a long time honing their skills before they succeeded. It is said that Ouyang Xun of the Tang Dynasty spent three days before a stone tablet that he was to write on. Wang Xizhi, the Sage of Calligraphy, turned a pond black after washing his brush in that pond for 20 years. That pond became known as the Ink Pond.

Before one can master the various writing styles in calligraphy, one should know the various strokes: dot, horizontal line, upstroke to the right, left-falling stroke, hook, bend, right-falling stroke and vertical line.

Ancient calligraphers practised with the character *yong* 永 because it encompasses all the eight basic strokes. Once you master this character, you will be able to grasp the strokes of Chinese characters in general.

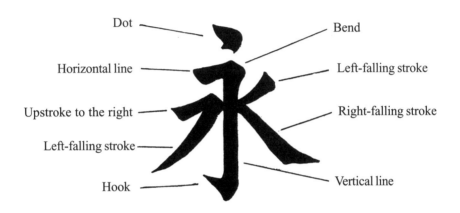

Dot

Horizontal line

Upstroke to the right

Left-falling stroke

Hook

Bend

Left-falling stroke

Right-falling stroke

Vertical line

The eight strokes of the character *yong*

Benefits of Calligraphy

One has to concentrate while writing calligraphy. Only then will his mind be at ease. He will then be at peace so that his intelligence and disposition can be enhanced.

Thus, calligraphy is not a mere art but also a psychological activity. Many calligraphers live to a ripe old age. This may be attributed to the benefits of calligraphy.

A Treasury of Calligraphy — The Stone Collection in Xi'an

Stone tablets appeared in China way back for the purpose of marking events. Hence one can find countless stone tablets left behind by the ancient people. In order to preserve some outstanding stone tablets, they were gathered together to form a repository of stone tablets. There are many repositories in China, with the one in Xi'an being the largest of them all.

The 1,000-odd stone tablets in Xi'an hailed from the Han to Qing Dynasties. Great calligraphers like Wang Xizhi, Yan Zhenqing, Liu Gongquan, Ouyang Xun, Zhang Xun and Huai Su had written on stone tablets. Xi'an thus became the favourite haunt for many a calligraphy enthusiast. The works of emperors like Tang Xuanzong, Song Weizong and Kangxi are also kept there.

The characters on the tablets can be preserved on paper. This is done by spreading a piece of thin paper on a tablet, and smoothing it out such that the characters can be seen jutting out. Lastly, apply ink to the paper. The characters on the tablets will thus be "printed' on the paper.

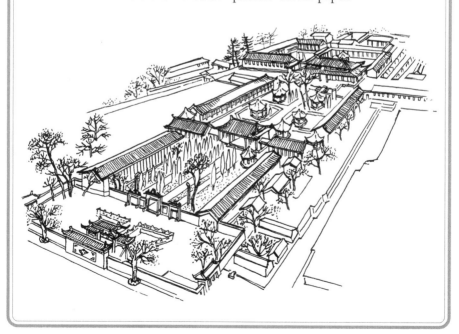

Appreciating Calligraphy

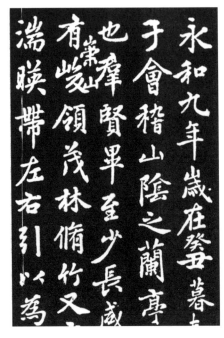

Wei-Jin Dynasties — Wang Xizhi
Orchid Pavilion Preface
This is Wang Xizhi's masterpiece and is hailed as the quintessential work of the *xingshu*. There are 324 characters. Repeated characters differ from one another. The character *zhi* alone has more than 20 styles.

Tang Dynasty — Ouyang Xun
Jiucheng Palace's Wine Fountain
Ouyang Xun created the irregular and quirky Ou-styled *kaishu*. He's hailed as one of four great Tang calligraphers. This piece of work combines both *lishu* and *kaishi*, and is firm yet gentle. It became the model for future generations where *kaishu* is concerned.

Tang Dynasty — Yan Zhenqing
A Tribute
Yan Zhenqing created the impactful Yan-styled *kaishu* which is powerful, vibrant and grand. *Ji Zhi Gao* is Yan Zhenqing's signature work. The strokes are continuous, earning this piece of calligraphy the title of the second best example of the *xingshu*.

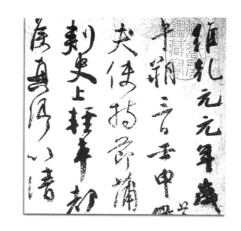

Tang Dynasty — Liu Gongquan
A Mystical Pagoda Stone
Liu Gongquan created a refreshing brand of *kaishu*. With his rich and ever-changing strokes, myriad of lines and a great force of imposing posture, he elevated the *kaishu* to greater heights.

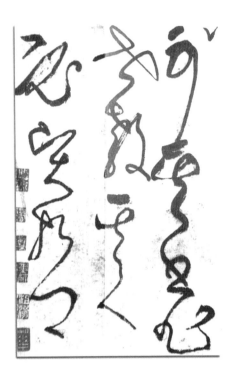

Tang Dynasty — Zhang Xu
Four Ancient Poems
Zhang Xu's works are the epitome of the *caoshu*. He's also known as the Sage of *Caoshu*. He loved his wine and often took up his brush when he was drunk. The unbridled style in *Gu Shi Si Tie* became his signature piece of work. It is also one of China's classics for the *caoshu*.

Tang Dynasty — Huai Su
An Ode to Self
Another master of the *caoshu*, Huai Su's strokes flow smoothly. Like a thunderstorm with its brilliant show of lightning and thunder, his unrestrained style brought the *caoshu* to a greater height.

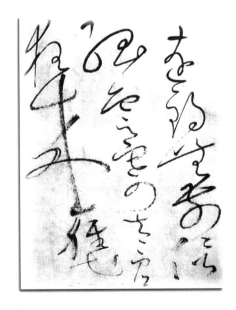

The Sage of Calligraphy
— Wang Xizhi

Wang Xizhi of the Eastern Jin Dynasty is the greatest calligrapher in Chinese history. All his brush strokes executed in the various styles were excellent. In addition, they all carried his own distinctive character and style. The annals of history hailed him as the Sage of Calligraphy.

When he was 12 years old...

Father, may I read this book on how to use a brush?

You're still young. You should be concentrating on your lessons with Madam Wei.

When you turn 20, I'll impart my skills to you.

Father, that will mean eight wasted years.

Father, please let me learn calligraphy now.

All right.

One month later…

Xizhi may be young, but his grasp of calligraphy is exceptional. I'm sure he will become a great calligrapher when he grows up.

When he grew up, Wang Xizhi continued to practise calligraphy relentlessly.

Your mouth is filled with ink!

Wang Xizhi's wife

Why are you eating a *mantou* smeared with ink?

Ha, ha... I was so carried away with my writing that I thought the *mantou* had been dipped in soup instead.

After every practice session, Wang Xizhi would wash his brush in the pond next to his house. As time passed by, the water in the pond turned blackish. It later became known as the famous Ink Pond.

Wang Xizhi was very fond of geese.

This pair of geese is so lovely.

Whether they're walking, running or swimming, their bodies and their necks coordinate so beautifully and perfectly. That's what calligraphy ought to be too!

Once, Wang Xizhi asked for a pair of geese from a Taoist priest. He spent half a day copying *Huang Ting Jing* 《黄庭经》, a Taoist book, using the small *kaishu*. This book later became the classic for the small *kaishu*.

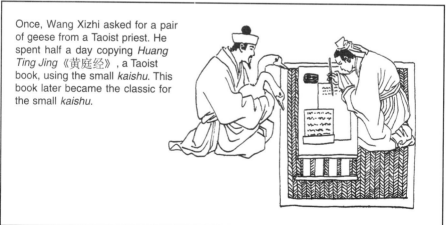

One day in late spring, when Wang Xizhi was 50 years old, he invited 41 calligraphy enthusiasts, poets, friends and relatives to a gathering at the Orchid Pavilion in Shaoxing, Zhejiang.

They sat by the two sides of a stream, on which lotus leaves filled with fine wine were floating. Once a lotus leaf cup reached someone, he had to make a poem on the spot. A total of 30 poems were composed.

Slightly tipsy, Wang Xizhi took up his brush and started putting down on paper all the poems of the day.

That writing, the *Orchid Pavilion Preface*, became the most outstanding piece of work for the *xingshu*. It had a far-reaching impact on Chinese calligraphy.

Eighteen Vats of Ink

Wang Xizhi's son, Wang Xianzhi, is also a well-known calligrapher. When Wang Xianzhi turned six, Wang Xizhi taught him calligraphy.

Let's see how he'll react when I take the brush away from him suddenly.

When you hold the brush, make sure that your posture is correct.

Yes, Father.

I don't believe you. I'm going to show it to Mother.

Mother, is my writing as good as Father's?

After eight years of learning calligraphy, you only manage to take on a little bit of your father's style.

This dot on the character *tai* does have your father's skill though.

...
...

Wang Xianzhi felt ashamed and continued to practise hard on his calligraphy. After using up the 18 vats of ink in the courtyard, he finally became a famous calligrapher during the Jin Dynasty.

Later generations spoke of him and his father in the same breath. They became known as the Two Wangs calligraphers.

CHAPTER *9*

PAINTING

Techniques in Chinese Painting

The techniques in Chinese painting may be classified into the following schools of styles: *gongbi* 工笔 (realistic or, literally, fine brushwork), *xieyi* 写意 (literally, write ideas) or a combination of both.

Gongbi painting
The brushstrokes are neat and attention is given to details.

Xieyi painting
The brushstrokes are less well-defined. Emphasis is placed on the overall expression and the painting is subject to the whim of the individual painter.

Expression

It is not easy to master Chinese painting. Other than good drawing skills, the air of the subject expressed through the brush strokes is given greater importance.

The eyes are the windows to one's soul. If the eyes of the subject are well drawn, the mien of the subject will come alive.

Gu Kaizi of the Eastern Jin Dynasty sometimes left out the eyes of his subject. He would take a few years before he filled in the eyes as he wanted to observe his subject in real life.

Colour

In Chinese paintings, the ink is the dominant feature while colours are peripheral. Chinese painters classify the black ink into five "colours":
- concentrated
- thick
- heavy
- thin
- light

Black is considered a colour and the varying intensity of its colour constitutes various colours.

Colours other than black are also used in Chinese painting. However, the way they are used is different from that seen in western painting. Western painting brings out the changing colours of a subject, depending on the light conditions.

Comparatively, Chinese painting only fills in the colour of the subject with no consideration given to varying light conditions. If there is any indication of changes, the same colour will be given different intensity for that purpose.

White Space

White spaces are often seen in Chinese painting. Though these spaces are left blank, they are still a part of the painting. They add life to the painting and give room for imagination.

A Blending of Components

Chinese painting is a marriage of poetry, calligraphy, seals and drawing. National artists often indicate the theme of the painting, the artist's name and the date of the painting.

At times, a poem or an extract from a prose is written next to the painting. These verses and lines complement and enrich the meaning behind the painting.

Seals are also affixed on the painting. They serve to embellish or balance the painting.

Calligraphy

Poetry

Drawing

Seal

Picture Mounting

Chinese paintings are also mounted to add brilliance to them. A painting that is not mounted is not considered to have been completed. Only Chinese paintings adhere to such a conviction. Different types of picture mounting are shown below.

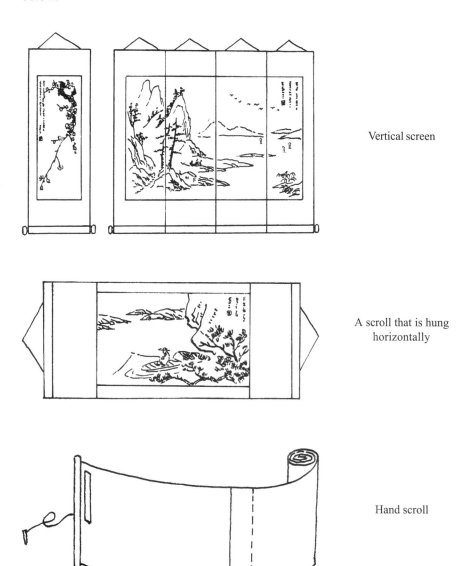

Vertical screen

A scroll that is hung horizontally

Hand scroll

The History of Chinese Painting

Modern Stone Age	Our ancestors began drawing on ceramic ware a long time ago. There were drawings of fish, deer, flowers and leaves.
Zhou, Qin, Eastern and Western Han Dynasties	Mural painting was popular and was often done in the form of portraits of famous people like Duke Zhou and Confucius. Lacquer ware painting, silk painting and stone painting of the Eastern and Western Han Dynasties are also well known.
Wei, Jin, Northern and Southern Dynasties	Painting became an art form. Great importance was attached to the disposition and mien of the subject in the paintings of Taoist priests, persons and portraitures. Painting of landscape was in the budding stage.
Sui and Tang Dynasties	This was the renaissance period for painting. Portraitures developed to become a specialty for the painting of palace maids. Paintings of landscape, flower-and-bird compositions and horses were also popular. Black ink superseded colours as the colour for painting. That set the norm and became a characteristic of folk painting.
Five Dynasties and Song Dynasties	Paintings of Taoist priests and people became less common. Flower-and-bird compositions and landscape took pride of place as the favourite subjects in painting.
Yuan, Ming and Qing Dynasties	Portraitures became even less common while paintings of landscape and flower-and-bird compositions were popular for a while. Retro painting was in and the emulation of styles was the mainstream.

Painting on stoneware during the Modern Stone Age

This is China's most famous and oldest silk painting. It depicts a dragon, a phoenix and a person during the Warring States Period.

These are *Paintings on Immortality* from the Eastern Han Dynasty.

The paintings in mausoleums during the Han Dynasty mostly depicted the attainment of immortality. This is a painting of Zhuang Yi and Nü Wa.

Categories of Chinese Painting

Landscape
Nature is the subject. It became another theme for painting during the Tang Dynasty. This form of painting developed most rapidly.

Bird-and-flower compositions
Flowers, grass, bamboo, stones, birds, animals, fish and insects are the main themes.

Portraiture
The subject is a person. This is the earliest type of painting in China.

Three Great Chinese Painters in Recent Times

Qi Baishi (1863-1957)

An outstanding calligrapher-cum-painter, he is known both at home and overseas. He is also known for his carving done in *zhuanshu*. His most famous works are his paintings of prawns, crabs and fishes.

Zhang Daqian (1899-1983)

A world-famous painter, Zhang Daqian made a name for himself at the young age of 30. In 1957, he was elected by the New York International Artists' Society as the greatest painter of his time. He was adept at painting landscape, people, flowers and birds. He was also a skilled calligrapher, poet and sculptor.

Xu Beihong (1895-1953)

He was a prominent painter and arts educator in China who held solo exhibitions in various parts of Europe. His forte lay in oil painting and Chinese painting. He was especially good at sketching and was known worldwide for his painting of horses.

Appreciating Chinese Painting

Tang Dynasty — Zhou Fang
Painting of Palace Maids
This is a depiction of imperial palace maids during the Tang Dynasty.

Song Dynasty — Guo Xi
Painting of an Early Spring
The queer pinnacles, unusual rocks, woods, pavilion and waterfall bring out the mood of spring.

Song Dynasty — Huang Jucai
Painting of a Mountain and Sparrows
This painting depicts an autumn scene. The sparrows are life-like and the painting brings out the richness of life.

Song Dynasty — Zhang Zeduan
Painting of River in Qingming
Painted on a long horizontal piece of paper, this historical painting portrays a bustling marketplace during the Song Dynasty. It provides a precious insight for academics studying the lives and times of the Song people. It is deemed as the masterpiece of realistic painting on ancient China.

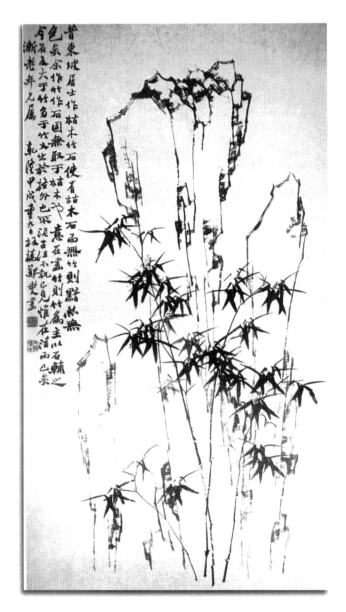

Qing Dynasty — Zheng Banqiao
Painting of Bamboo
This work is a wonderful coming-together of calligraphy and drawing. It is both "calligraphy and painting in action".

The Father of Painting
— Wu Daozi

Wu Daozi was a famous painter from the Tang Dynasty. He is also known as the Sage of Painting and the Forefather of Painting.

He is best known for his painting of Zhong Kui catching ghosts for Emperor Tang Xuanzong.

It is said that Tang Xuanzong was in dreamland one night...

You evil imp, you have nowhere to run!

A little ghost was carrying Tang Xuanzong's robe and one of Yang Guifei's jade pieces while a bigger ghost was hot on its heels, running in circles inside Tang Xuanzong's chamber.

Tang Xuanzong was so shaken by the dream that he fainted.

Since that night, Tang Xuanzong had been unable to eat and sleep. He soon fell ill.

What worries me is whether the big ghost has caught the little ghost.

Why don't we get someone to paint the two ghosts in Your Majesty's dream?

We will then use it to make inquiries among the masses.

Tang Xuanzong summoned the most famous painter of that time, Wu Daozi, to the palace.

Your Majesty, was this the big ghost you saw in your dream?

Ah!

Oh no! I have accidentally smeared a stroke across the painting.

This stroke happens to land in the hand of the big ghost. It looks like he's holding a sword in his hand.

I'll hang this painting in my private chamber.

That very night, Tang Xuanzong again dreamt of the big ghost. This time, he brandished a sword and slashed the little ghost into two.

I may set my mind at ease now.

Tang Xuanzong bestowed the title of God of Painting on Wu Daozi and put him in charge of the paintings of Buddha for the Luoyang Temple in Chang'an.

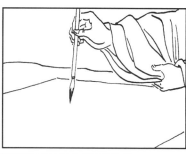

Mr Wu, please draw a pair of lions for me. I'd like to use them as a reference for my stone lion sculpture.

That's easy.

It's done. You may have it.

It is said that Wu Daozi never completed his paintings for fear that his drawings would come alive.

Mr Wu, you've forgotten to draw the eyes.

Once I do that, the lions will come to life.

That can't be. You look down on me, a mere stone sculptor, so you're unwilling to complete the painting.

Wu Daozi had no choice but to draw the eyes as well.

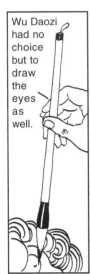

Without its eyes, the lion went back into the painting.

It's really come alive! And it's hurt my donkey!

The sculptor quickly gouged out the beast's eyes with his tools.

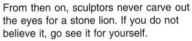

From then on, sculptors never carve out the eyes for a stone lion. If you do not believe it, go see it for yourself.

CHAPTER *10*

CHINESE NEW YEAR PICTURE

There is another kind of painting in China which is known as *nianhua* 年画 (New Year pictures). The common folk will paste these pictures on their doors or walls during the Chinese Lunar New Year to mark the auspicious festival. If you paste a *nianhua* in your house, do remember to replace it with a new one for the coming year. Welcoming the new is the Chinese way of ushering in the new year or new spring.

Pasting *nianhua* during New Year adds to the festivity.

When Man was still living in caves, there were no doors for him to decorate with. When Man moved into houses, he still feared the poisonous snakes and wild beasts. So he pasted on his doors pictures and symbols signifying power over evil forces. These pictures could be considered the earliest type of *nianhua*.

In the early days, pictures were pasted on doors to ward off evil. That was how the practice of pasting *nianhua* began.

These door gods certainly look fierce! With this picture on the door, all demons will flee!

The earliest *nianhua* depicted door gods and were believed to ward off evil. *Nianhua* originated among the common folk. They reflect the desires and wishes of the commoner. During the Tang and Song Dynasties, *nianhua* which were both decorative and which expressed one's desires emerged.

A *nianhua* of door gods

The Various Themes in *Nianhua*

Life of the commoner
A farmer at work, a fisherman's joy, harvest time, New Year, celebration of the 15ᵗʰ day of the lunar month, etc

Stories from history
Yue Fei and his patriotism, Dou Yan teaching her son, Emperor Qianlong's Jiangnan tour, etc

Mythical legends
Chang E flying to the moon, Madam White Snake, etc

Joyous occasions
Five boys passing the imperial examinations, a good harvest, prosperity, peace all year round, etc; they reflect the people's pursuit of a good life

Deities
God of Fortune, Guan Yu (Warrior God), etc

Humourous and satirical
A mouse marrying off his daughter, a mantis getting married, etc

Babies
Nianhua with babies as the theme expresses the people's wish to perpetuate their family lineage and the traditional notion of and desire for a large family

Nianhua with various themes

The Development of *Nianhua*

Nianhua later spread to Japan, England, France and Southeast Asia. It was very well-received in those places.

Calendars with *nianhua* and hanging calendars even made their appearance whereby calendars and *nianhua* were combined. Block printing was employed. The calendars were pretty and very popular among the people.

There are many sects in *nianhua*:

Area	Specialty
Yangliuqing, Tianjin	Intricate, elegant
Beijing	Rugged
Huai County, Shandong	Rugged and loud
Taohuawu, Suzhou	Exquisite and simple
Zhangzhou, Fujian	Powder printing in black
Foshan	Black picture on red background

Paper Cutting

There is another type of *nianhua* which is not called *nianhua* but *chuanghua* 窗花 (literally, window flowers). It is a form of paper cutting and has a long history. The womenfolk in the northern part of China would gather together to do this craft just before New Year. A pair of scissors was all that they needed to cut out pretty and intricate designs to be pasted on the windows.

Like *nianhua*, *chuanghua* is not only pretty and adds to the festivity, it also implies ushering in happiness and good luck. The themes in *chuanghua* are often flowers, domesticated animals, characters in operas or myths and legends.

Spring Couplet

During New Year, spring couplets are another favourite item that people will put up. Spring couplets are also known as matching couplets. They are written on paper and cloth or carved on bamboo, wood and pillars. The couplets have to match each other in terms of presentation and content. Spring couplets were already seen during the Five Dynasties. Come the Song Dynasty, it was a common feature and has been so until this day.

Spring couplets convey the people's pursuit of a good and happy life. Couplets were also common in everyday life.

Characters and matching couplets are also often seen on the pillars of buildings, tombstones, temple pavilions, scenic spots. These are not called spring couplets. They are further categorised into longevity couplets, elegiac couplets, congratulatory couplets, scenic spot couplets, residence couplets and many more.

Connected characters are also seen on buildings and scenic spots.

Among the commoners, a single piece of paper with characters on it was also commonly seen. For example, *ru kou ping an* 入口平安 (safety) is pasted at home and *fei zhu man quan* 肥猪满圈 (a sty full of fat pigs) is pasted outside the pigsty.

Alternatively, single characters like *chun* 春 (spring), *fu* 福 (happiness) and *cai* 财 (fortune) are also seen. They are pasted upside down (*dao* 倒) to denote *chun dao* 春到 (spring is here) or *fu dao* 福到 (happiness is here).

Happiness is here!

Appreciating *Nianhua*

Qing Dynasty — Yangliuqing
Deity Bestowing Good Fortune

Qing Dynasty — Yangliuqing
Peace Throughout the Four Seasons
Four adorable children carrying a vase (*ping* 瓶) of flowers each. There are peonies, lotus flowers, chrysanthemums and tea flowers, with each depicting a different season. The picture therefore symbolises peace (*ping* 平) all year round.

Qing Dynasty — Yangliuqing
Unicorn Bestowing a Child
This picture depicts the people's desire for many offspring.

Qing Dynasty — Yangliuqing
Year After Year of Abundance
Using the pun from lotus flower (*lian* 莲) and fish (*yu* 鱼), a picture depicting year after year (*lian nian* 连年) of abundance (*yu* 余) is formed.

Yangliuqing's New Year Pictures

During Qianlong's reign in the Qing Dynasty, there was a female painter called Bai Junying in Xiyang County, Tianjin. Her New Year picture *Nian Nian You Yu* (yearly abundance) was very popular.

Sir, this is the painting, *Nian Nian You Yu,* that you wanted.

I come from Shengfang Town. Since I'm here, I thought I'd buy a painting home.

Dear, I'm home. Look, I've even bought a New Year picture.

This little fat child looks so alert. The lotus flowers are so lovely and the many golden carp are so life-like.

I can never get tired of this painting.

Grandpa and Grandma, bring me a wooden basin. I'll catch fishes for you.

The child in the painting can talk!

Let's do as the child says.

On the second day...

Old man, come here, quick!

Look, what a fresh carp!

If only we could have this fish every day.
My dear child, one fish is not enough. Give me 10 fishes.
On the following day…
There are 10 big carp in the wooden basin!
We can't possibly finish them all. Let's sell them.
Ha, ha, we've made quite a tidy sum.

CHAPTER *11*

MUSIC

Chinese music has a long history and is believed to have made its appearance some 7,000 years ago.

Music in Religious Rituals

Music was first closely linked to religious rituals. Musicians during that time were sorcerers. During the Zhou Dynasty, *liuyue* 六乐 was offered as a sacrifice unto Heaven and Earth, the sun and the moon, mountains and rivers and forefathers.

Liuyue refers to the music of ancient emperors like the Yellow Emperor, Yao and Shun, and that of the Xia, Shang and Zhou Dynasties.

Music and Politics

Duke Zhou of the Zhou Dynasty created rituals and music, making music one of the two main pillars in maintaining order. At that time, music had heavy political undertones. Officials, great and small, all had their own orchestras. The arrangement of music and the number of musicians were based on the rank of the official. For example, the emperor's musicians formed four sides and the dance troupe had eight persons in each of the eight rows. As for the highest-ranking official in the land, he would have musicians forming three sides with four persons in each of the four rows.

Music and the Expression of Emotions

When it came to the Wei, Jin, Northern and Southern Dynasties, Chinese music became an expression of one's thoughts and emotions.

Characteristics of Chinese Music

Chinese music has unique characteristics. It has contrasting styles of fast or slow tempo and tight or loose arrangement, thereby communicating an air and temperament that is balanced, peaceful and simple. In addition, Chinese music reflects the moderate nature of Chinese philosophy.

Confucius and Music

Confucius was not just a great philosopher and educator. He was also an outstanding musician. He had such a great love for music that though he encountered many difficulties during his tour of the states, he never stopped playing music.

When he heard the ancient melody *Shao* 韶 in the state of Qi, he was so mesmerised by it that he could go without meat for three months.

Confucius believed in the political and educational components of music. He emphasised the marriage of rituals and music, which he felt would help in changing established habits and social customs and in maintaining law and order.

Confucius attached great importance to the moral integrity of music. He believed that music should be guided by moral values and opposed strongly to the pure enjoyment of music. His ideal music was one that is not too self-indulgent and excessive in emotions.

Chinese Musical Instruments

Chinese musical instruments have at least 7,000 years of history. During the Zhou Dynasty about 3,000 years ago, there were around 70 instruments. Today, there are hundreds of Chinese musical instruments around. They can be broadly categorised into string, percussion and wind.

Guqin 古琴

It is the king of ancient Chinese musical instruments. It was already seen during the Zhou Dynasty. It is a type of stringed instrument with five strings originally. Music is made by plucking the strings. It was not until the Wei and Jin Dynasties that the seven-stringed version became the standard. The *guqin* has strong resonant sounds, can play a wide repertoire and is highly versatile. It is suitable for powerful and grand pieces as well as soft and gentle ones. It has a deep yet reticent timbre not present in other musical instruments.

Zheng 箏

It was very popular during the Qin Dynasty. Generally, the *zheng* has 12 or 13 strings. It is especially suited for mimicking the sounds of waves and howling winds.

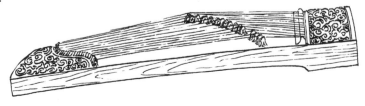

Pipa 琵琶

It is said that *pipa* originated in Persia. It was brought into China around the fourth century from the western region. The way *pipa* is plucked is mainly derived from that of *guqin*. However, it has its own distinctions. The *pipa* is highly versatile — it can produce the sounds of 10,000 horses, melancholic pieces as well as light-hearted and happy melodies.

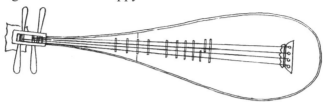

Erhu 二胡

It is a stringed instrument that evolved from the *xiqin* 奚琴, *jiqin* 嵇琴 and *huqin* 胡琴 of the Tang and Song Dynasties. The sounds of the *erhu* are ever-changing. It can play both soft as well as vibrant pieces. Many a Chinese opera uses *erhu* as its main musical accompaniment.

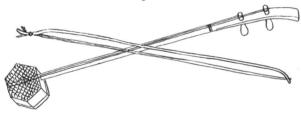

Xiao 簫

The earliest version was the *paixiao* 排簫 where many tubes were arranged together. Each tube would produce a distinct sound. It was made obsolete during the Song and Yuan Dynasties. The *xiao* we see today is a variation of the *qiangdi* 羌笛 from the Han Dynasty. It is made of a single tube. It was originally a musical instrument among the minority ethnic groups. The sound of the *xiao* is light and elegant. It complements the *guqin* especially well. It is a favourite among people who choose to live in the deep woods and mountains.

Di 笛

The *di* produces clear, loud, elated and passionate sounds. It is excellent for conveying elation and joy. The making of a *di* is simple and low in cost, hence it is a popular instrument among the common people.

Yangqin 扬琴

This is a percussion instrument. Its composition is more complicated and is made of three major parts: the frame, the strings and the keys. The sounds it produces are reverberant and strong yet soft. It blends in easily with other musical instruments.

Bianzhong 编钟

This percussion instrument is made of bells in various sizes. The bell is hollow and on each bell is carved the face of an animal. The *bianzhong* comes in various forms according to the number of bells. The number of bells can be nine, 13, 16, 64 and so on. The sound of the *bianzhong* is similar to that of a bell — clear, pristine and lingering.

The Top Ten Chinese Musical Pieces

Towering Hills and Flowing Streams	A *guqin* piece that highlights the movement of rivers and the myriad of mountains
Plum Blossoms	A famed *guqin* piece which describes the plum blossom that takes its pride of place despite the chilly snow and frost
Admiring Flowers by the Moonlit River	A *pipa* piece; like a piece of painting, it is a blend of scenery and emotions, movement amidst stillness
Autumn Moon Over Han Palace	An *erhu* piece; a melancholic piece that depicts the sorrows of a palace maid
Springtime After Winter	A *pipa* piece; light and fast-paced, it speaks of the lively springtime after a gloomy winter
Dialogue Between Fisherman and Woodcutter	A light and easy piece that reflects a recluse's desire for the life of a fisherman
18 Beats of the Reed Pipe	A sorrowful and sad piece that tells the story of Cai Wenchen of the Han Dynasty who was enslaved by the Huns; it depicts his tribulations and thoughts of his homeland
Guang Lin San	A *guqin* piece; a passionate piece that describes Nie Zheng's assassination of the emperor of Han
Wild Geese Flying ACross the Desert	A light-hearted and easy *guqin* piece; by depicting a picture of a flock of wild geese, it expresses a person's ambition
Ambush From 10 Directions	A *pipa* piece played on a grand scale with great energy and robustness of spirit; it describes the fierce battle between Chu and Han

The Legend of Shi Kuang

Shi Kuang was a famous musician during the Spring and Autumn Period. He was blind. Jin Wengong enjoyed his performance tremendously.

I love melancholic pieces. Play a most melancholic piece for me*.

It's far too melancholic. I'm afraid it won't do Your Majesty good to hear it.

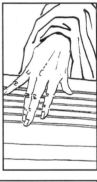

Sigh...

It's only a melody. What harm can it do to me? Play it.

Your music is so heartbreaking...

Being overwhelmed by emotions, Jin Wengong could not bring himself to eat that day.

Soon after, he was taken ill.

Your Majesty, looks like I have to cure you of your malady.

Shi Kuang, do you have a way out?

Shi Kuang started playing a light-hearted piece of music.

Your music seems to depict a spring morning after a storm.

The grief in my heart is gone. I've recovered!

From then on, word spread that Shi Kuang's music could resurrect a dead person.

Until this day, a band will accompany a funeral procession in the hope that the dead will be resurrected.

Though no one has ever come back to life in this manner, people still believe that the music serves to appease the soul of the dead person.

Shi Kuang was not only well versed in playing the *qin*, he had sharp ears for music too. There was a time when the states of Jin and Chu were engaged in a war.

Your Majesty, someone from the Chu camp is playing the *qin*.

Is that so? Let's go and check it out. See if he plays well.

Indeed. Someone is playing the *qin*.

But he doesn't play it as well as you do.

Congratulations, Your Majesty.

Why are you congratulating me?

Music speaks of one's heart. I can hear that the music is desolate and lacks fighting spirit. The Chu army is therefore low in morale.

If our army invades them now, victory will be ours.

Indeed. The morale of an army is very important in a war.

Jin Wengong followed Shi Kuang's advice and invaded the enemy's camp. As expected, they defeated the Chu army.

Jin Wengong thought very highly of Shi Kuang's ability and conferred him the title of God of Music. Orchestras and musicians of later generations all regarded Shi Kuang as their predecessor.

CHAPTER *12*

WEIQI

Weiqi is a traditional Chinese chess game. It's said that *weiqi* was invented by Yao, who used it to coach his son Danzhu. *Weiqi* had already gained popularity during the Warring States Period.

Yao, the mythical ancient holy emperor, teaching his son *weiqi*

Men of ancient China
enjoying a game of *weiqi*

An international *weiqi* competition

Weiqi was introduced into Japan during the Later Tang Dynasty. It was even incorporated into the Japanese culture. In the 19th century, *weiqi* was introduced to Europe. During the 1980s, more than 10 countries from the Asian, European and American continents organised a *weiqi* competition. Various countries also hold *weiqi* competitions and seminars. *Weiqi* has become a bridge for international cultural exchanges.

The ancient people called *weiqi* "*shoutan*" or "*zuoyin*". *Shoutan* 手谈 means chatting by using one's hands. Though no words are exchanged during the chess game, one can still read the thoughts and moods of the other party.

Zuoyin 坐隐 refers to two persons having a chat while seated together. The seeds on the chess board express both parties' strategies, feelings, moods and motives.

As such, *weiqi* is a game whereby two people attempt to expose each other's intentions. One's style of game reflects one's personality. Thus, *weiqi* reveals a person's character and mentality.

Chess Professors and Chess Officials

During the Tang Dynasty, the palace even appointed a chess professor and chess official. The former was in charge of coaching while the latter would wait on the emperor and high-ranking officials while they had their game of *weiqi*.

Chess Equipment

Chessboard

There are 19 horizontal and 19 vertical lines crossing each other to form 361 intersection points. The intersection point is known as *qi* 气. Nine of these points are highlighted and are known as the *xingwei* 星位 (star positions). The central star position is called the *tianyuan* 天元. There are also chessboards with 13 or 9 lines across, suitable for beginners.

Xingwei　　*Tianyuan*

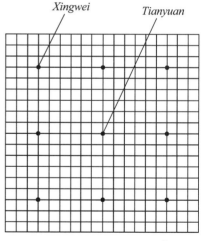

Seeds

They come in black and white. There are 180 white seeds and 181 black seeds. Altogether, there are 361 seeds.

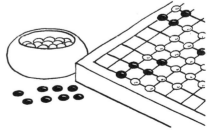

Rules of the Game

Weiqi is all about invading space. The party holding the majority of the chessboard with his seeds is the winner.

1. There are two players. One takes the white seeds while the other, the black seeds.
2. The one with the black seeds starts the game by placing his seed on any intersection point on the chessboard.
3. The player with the white seed will then place his. The first player will then place his second black seed and the game goes on in this way.
4. At the end of the game, the player with the most number of his seeds on the chessboard is the winner.

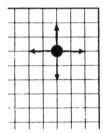 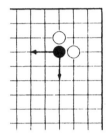

1. When one seed is blocked by the opponent's seed on one side, thus impeding its advancement, this seed has lost one *qi*.

2. When the opponent's seed or seeds surround one's seed such that there is only one available *qi* left, that seed is being placed in a position where it will soon be "checkmated".

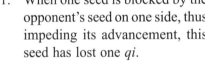

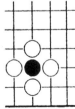 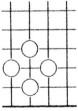 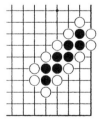 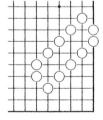

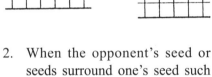

3. When the opponent's seeds surround the seed on all sides, it shall be removed from the board.

4. In the above diagram, white seeds are surrounding the black seeds. The white seeds thus gain more space on the board.

Stages in *Weiqi*

Learning how to play *weiqi* is easy but mastering it is not. *Weiqi* involves many manoeuvres. In a game of *weiqi*, there are three stages, namely *buju*, *zhongpan zhandou* and *guanzi*. Every stage has its own important manoeuvres.

Buju 布局

Both parties establish their territories in the corners and sides of the board. They will try to take up strategic points on the board so that they can control the seeds.

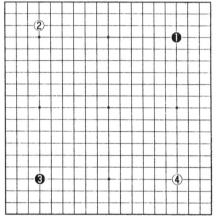

Black seeds 1 and 3 and white seeds 2 and 4 face each other. This is a common strategy.

Zhongpan 中盘

The seeds advance towards the centre of the board such that both parties will gain and lose along the way. After a fierce battle, the territory of each colour is soon established.

Guanzi 官子

Both parties attempt to expand its territory while decreasing the opponent's until all the intersection points are occupied.

At the end of a game, the number of each colour seed is counted to decide the winner.

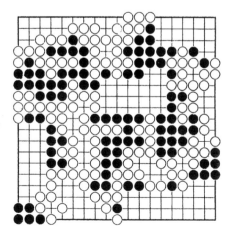

The Nine-Part System of *Weiqi*

The ancient judiciary system had nine ranks in all. Even the arts have a ranking system where paintings and calligraphy are ranked *shenpin* 神品, *miaopin* 妙品 and *nengpin* 能品. Each category has three classes. This ranking system is known as "three grades, nine classes".

In ancient times, *weiqi* players were ranked under the nine-grade system. Since the Ming and Qing Dynasties, players have been ranked as *guoshou* 国手, *ershou* 二手, *sanshou* 三手 and *sishou* 四手. Again, each grade is further divided into various classes. In all, there are about nine classes. The Japanese also emulated this ranking system. The world over now adopts this nine-part ranking system.

Let me show you the hand gestures.

Hand Gestures

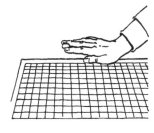

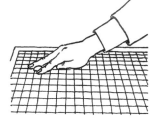

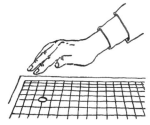

1. The seed is held between the index finger and middle finger.

2. The seed is placed in the intersection point.

3. The hand moves away from the board.

Who Gets to Use the White or Black Seeds?

How do we decide who gets to take the black seeds? Usually, the less competent player will take the black seeds while the better player, the white seeds.

If both players are evenly matched or if they are playing together for the first time, they will hold a guessing game to decide who takes the black seeds.

Player A will hold a few seeds in his hand. Player B will then guess if the number of seeds is an even or odd number.

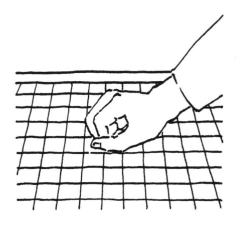

Player A will then count the seeds in his hand. If Player B's guess is correct, B will take the black seeds while A, the white seeds. If B makes a wrong guess, the converse will happen.

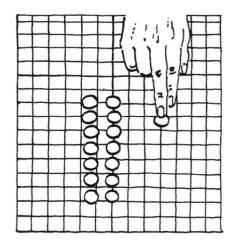

Li Shimin Versus Jia Yuan

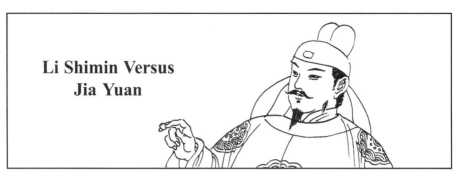

The Tang emperor, Li Shimin, played a mean game of *weiqi*. All the *weiqi* experts would have a game of *weiqi* with him in the capital. One of these men was the highly-skilled Jia Yuan. The emperor especially enjoyed having a game with him.

Jia Yuan, you're not an honest man.

Why do you always lose to me?

That is because Your Majesty is too highly skilled. I just cannot beat you.

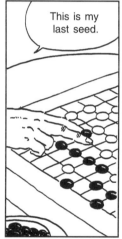

Wait. I let you have an advantage of two seeds. That means I've beaten you by one seed.

You've lost.

Men, take him to the puddle of water!

Your Majesty, halt! There is one more seed in my palm.

Ha, ha, ha!

You won't claim victory unless you're driven into a corner.

Your Majesty is brilliant.

CHAPTER *13*

XIANGQI

Other than *weiqi*, there is another chess game that is very popular — *xiangqi*.

Xiangqi is a traditional Chinese chess game. A chessboard and pawns are involved in the game.

Chess Equipment

Chessboard

It consists of nine vertical lines and 10 horizontal lines. There are 99 meeting points on the board. The pawns are placed in these red points.

There is a middle section on the board that is not marked with lines. It is called the river. The area marked with a cross is the Nine Palace.

Pawns

There are 32 pawns which are divided into red and black ones. Each colour group has 16 pawns which are further divided into seven types.

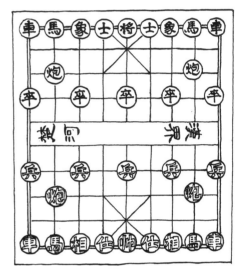

The red pawns comprise one commander-in-chief, one chariot, one horse, one cannon, one premier, two scholars and five soldiers.

The black pawns constitute one general, one chariot, one horse, one cannon, one elephant, two scholars and five soldiers.

Each pawn has different moves.

Chessboard and pawns for *xiangqi*

Procedures

In a game of *xiangqi*, the players will place their pawns in their rightful positions. The player with the red pawns makes the first move. Both parties will take turns to make their moves until one's general or commander-in-chief is "killed" or the game ends in a stalemate.

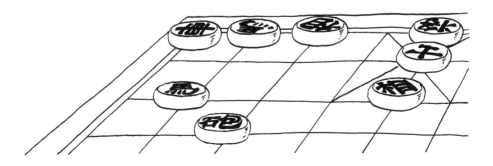

The Development of *Xiangqi*

Xiangqi already existed during the Warring States Period. The earliest type of *xiangqi* pawns were made of gold-plated copper figurines of horses and soldiers. Hence it was called *xiang* (resemblance) *qi*. It has nothing to do with elephants (*xiang*) at all. As this type of chess pieces was expensive, only royalty and aristocrats could afford to play the game.

During the Tang Dynasty, wooden figurines made their appearance. That was when *xiangqi* became a popular game among the common people.

After the downfall of the Qin Dynasty, the states of Chu and Han engaged in a fierce battle. Liu Bang of Han and Xiang Yu of Chu used a man-made river to demarcate the boundary. Later generations added this man-made river to the chessboard, naming it River Chu and Han Boundary.

The Origins of 3-D Figurines

During the chaotic times in the Tang Dynasty, Emperor Tangming escaped to Sichuan. The entourage ran into a heavy storm and took shelter in a small inn. Crown Prince Li Heng and his favourite concubine played chess to kill boredom. At that time, the copper figurines made a lot of noise on the board. Premier Li Mi advised the Crown Prince, "If all you do is engage in *xiangqi*, you will incur the unhappiness of the army."

Li Heng thus ordered that the chess pawns be made of a soft wood so that he could continue with his game. From then on, wooden *xiangqi* pawns became a regular feature.

Towards the end of the Tang Dynasty, the Chinese people invented the first cannon ball. It became a new war weapon and was incorporated into *xiangqi*.

The system of *xiangqi* underwent a major revamp during the Northern Song Dynasty. The layout of the chessboard, the names of the pawns and the rules of the game were reinvented. That established the popular *xiangqi* as we know it today.

After the rules of the game and the chessboard were established, copper or wooden round pieces with characters printed on them gradually replaced 3-D pawns. Today, such pawns are still in use.

Interesting *Xiangqi* Jargon

Cannon on the Heels of the Horse

The horse is one square away from the enemy's general or commander-in-chief on the same line, thus immobilising the latter. The cannon is then placed behind the horse and "checkmates" the opponent by leaping over the horse. This refers to a move that comes too late.

Offering a Toast With Two Cups

One party uses a pair of cannons to hit out at the opponent's elephant in the rear.

Seeing Buddha Home

One party uses his soldiers to force the opponent's general or commander-in-chief back to the starting point to clinch victory.

Deity Showing the Way

An opening move that allows one party to test the enemy's strategy by using soldiers to open a way through for the horse.

Xiangqi has no lack of interesting jargon. They describe the moves made in *xiangqi* most aptly.

The Legend of Mt Lanke

During the Jin Dynasty, a woodcutter by the name of Wang Qiao lived at the foot of a mountain in Xin'an County of He'nan.

These two children play the game very well. I'll watch them for a while before I go back.

Wang Qiao was held spellbound by the game...

Grr...

Hungry? Eat this.

Thank you.

But would this small fruit fill my stomach?

After eating the fruit, Wang Qiao did not feel hungry or thirsty at all. He stayed on to watch 30 more rounds of the game.

We've been out for a long time.

Teacher will be back soon. Let's go back.

One of the children waved towards the skies.

Don't tell me they're deities?!

So the axe is here.

This is strange. The axe has become rusty and the handle is broken.

Wang Qiao is back!

It's Wang Qiao indeed!

Wang Qiao later found out that he had been away for three years. He told his fellow villagers the amazing encounter he had had.

He even showed them the game plan.

That's an amazing game. It's not something that the ordinary man is capable of. You must have run into deities.

No wonder you said you only stayed in the cave for a short time when three years have passed in the mundane world. Why don't you record the games you witnessed and leave it as a legacy for future generations?

Let's call the book *Lan Futou Ba Er Xiangqi Pu.*

That's too long. Let's call the axe *ke.* We'll call it the *Lan Ke Zhen Ji (The Broken Axe* Xiangqi *Manual).*

This book has been passed down till this day. Later generations called that mountain Mt Lanke and the cave, Wang Qiao Dong.

A Brief Chronology of Chinese History

夏 Xia Dynasty			About 2100 – 1600 BC
商 Shang Dynasty			About 1600 – 1100 BC
周 Zhou Dynasty	西周 Western Zhou Dynasty		About 1100 – 771 BC
	東周 Eastern Zhou Dynasty		770 – 256 BC
	春秋 Spring and Autumn Period		770 – 476 BC
	戰國 Warring States		475 – 221 BC
秦 Qin Dynasty			221 – 207 BC
漢 Han Dynasty	西漢 Western Han		206 BC – AD 24
	東漢 Eastern Han		25 – 220
三國 Three Kingdoms	魏 Wei		220 – 265
	蜀漢 Shu Han		221 – 263
	吳 Wu		222 – 280
西晉 Western Jin Dynasty			265 – 316
東晉 Eastern Jin Dynasty			317 – 420
南北朝 Northern and Southern Dynasties	南朝 Southern Dynasties	宋 Song	420 – 479
		齊 Qi	479 – 502
		梁 Liang	502 – 557
		陳 Chen	557 – 589
	北朝 Northern Dynasties	北魏 Northern Wei	386 – 534
		東魏 Eastern Wei	534 – 550
		北齊 Northern Qi	550 – 577
		西魏 Western Wei	535 – 556
		北周 Northern Zhou	557 – 581
隋 Sui Dynasty			581 – 618
唐 Tang Dynasty			618 – 907
五代 Five Dynasties	後梁 Later Liang		907 – 923
	後唐 Later Tang		923 – 936
	後晉 Later Jin		936 – 946
	後漢 Later Han		947 – 950
	後周 Later Zhou		951 – 960
宋 Song Dynasty	北宋 Northern Song Dynasty		960 – 1127
	南宋 Southern Song Dynasty		1127 – 1279
遼 Liao Dynasty			916 – 1125
金 Jin Dynasty			1115 – 1234
元 Yuan Dynasty			1271 – 1368
明 Ming Dynasty			1368 – 1644
清 Qing Dynasty			1644 – 1911
中華民國 Republic of China			1912 – 1949
中華人民共和國 People's Republic of China			1949 –

CHINESE CULTURE SERIES

150x210mm, 160-192 pages, fully illustrated

ORIGINS OF CHINESE MUSIC
The origins and characteristics of Chinese musical instruments are explored, covering Chinese music from prehistoric era to the modern times.
ISBN 978-981-229-475-3

ORIGINS OF CHINESE NAMES
Find out the origins of 100 Chinese family names, and understand how Chinese names are chosen to reflect the customs and beliefs of the times.
ISBN 978-981-229-462-3

ORIGINS OF CHINESE PEOPLE & CUSTOMS
Explores the beginnings of the Chinese people, origins of Chinese names, Chinese zodiac signs, the afterlife, social etiquette and more!
ISBN 981-229-384-1

ORIGINS OF CHINESE FESTIVALS
Stories about Lunar New Year, Chinese Valentine's Day, Qing Ming, Dragon Boat, Zhong Yuan, Mid-Autumn Festivals and more.
ISBN 981-229-378-7

ORIGINS OF CHINESE CULTURE
Interesting facts about the "Four Treasures of the Study": the brush, ink, paper and inkstone, which form the cornerstone of Chinese culture.
ISBN 981-229-407-4

ORIGINS OF CHINESE ART AND CRAFT
Packed with information on artistic interests covering Chinese embroidery, lacquerware, paper cutting, face masks and pottery.
ISBN 981-229-441-4

ORIGINS OF CHINESE MARTIAL ARTS
Explores the *gongfu* of Shaolin and Wudang warriors, their philosophy and chivalry code.
ISBN 981-229-268-3

ORIGINS OF SHAOLIN KUNG FU
The monks of Shaolin Temple have become synonymous with Chinese martial arts while cultivating the virtues of Buddhism.
ISBN 981-229-408-2

ORIGINS OF CHINESE CUISINE
Showcases famous and best-relished dishes like Peking Roast Duck and Buddha Jumps Over the Wall, and the stories behind them.
ISBN 981-229-317-5

ORIGINS OF CHINESE FOOD CULTURE
Covers the origins, history, customs, and the art and science of Chinese food culture, including the 18 methods of cooking.
ISBN 981-229-318-3

ORIGINS OF CHINESE TEA AND WINE
Explores the origins, history, customs and art of Chinese tea and wine, including stories of how famous varieties of tea and wine came to be.
ISBN 981-229-369-8

ORIGINS OF CHINESE SCIENCE & TECHNOLOGY
Covers great inventions by the Chinese: the compass, paper-making, gunpowder and printing. Explores their expertise in geography, mathematics and agriculture.
ISBN 981-229-376-0

ORIGINS OF TIBETAN CULTURE
Explore the origins of the Tibetan sky burial, the reverence of the Dalai Lama and folk beliefs.
ISBN 981-229-314-0

HISTORY

Imperial Chinese Women

The harem was a place where only the most beautiful, intelligent, fortunate and ruthless women could rise to the top. This book tells the stories of these women, the outstanding, the outrageous, the glorious and the tragic ones of the Chinese imperial harem.

160pp, ISBN 978-981-229-482-1

NEW

Chinese History: Ancient China to 1911

This book will help you to comprehend and interpret China's history in its proper context, plus provide vivid illustrations, and questions and answers to enhance your appreciation of great people and happenings.

192pp, ISBN 981-229-439-2

Great Chinese Emperors: Tales of Wise and Benevolent Rule

Read the tales of wise and benevolent rulers including Shennong, Li Shimin (Tang dynasty) and Emperor Kangxi (Qing dynasty). These stand tall for their outstanding contributions and character.

192pp, ISBN 981-229-451-1

Infamous Chinese Emperors: Tales of Tyranny and Misrule

Stories of China's most notorious emperors who are a motley crew of squanderers, murderers, thugs and lechers, and how they got their just deserts!

192pp, ISBN 981-229-459-7

PHILOSOPHY

ZEN INSPIRATION
Zen is a way of creative living. In this book, you will find out about Zen in all its vitality and simplicity. Whatever it is about Zen that fascinates you – silent meditation or creative expression – you will not be disappointed as you dip into the pages of this book.
Illustrated by **Fu Chunjiang**. *224pp, 150x210mm, ISBN 981-229-455-4.*

INSPIRATION FROM CONFUCIUS:
Choice Quotations from the Analects
More than 100 choice quotations classified under broad themes depicting Confucian core values and enhanced by inspirational thoughts. With additional features on Confucius' life, achievements and influence, it makes an excellent representation of the *Analects*.
Illustrated by **Jeffrey Seow**. *224pp, 150x210mm, ISBN 981-229-398-1.*

THE TAO INSPIRATION :
Essence of Lao Zi's Wisdom
Written more than 2,500 years ago, the Tao Te Ching now comes in 21st century style. Presenting Lao Zi's masterpiece in a concise, comprehensive yet profound manner, this book provides practical wisdom for leadership and for achieving balance and harmony in everyday life.
Illustrated by **Feng Ge**. *176pp, 150x210mm, ISBN 981-229-396-5.*

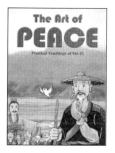

THE ART OF PEACE
The perfect companion if daily stories on war and terrorism are tiring you out. Learn how Mo Zi spread his message of peace to warring states locked in endless conflicts and power struggles.
Illustrated by **Chan Kok Sing**, *152pp, 150x210mm, ISBN 981-229-390-6.*

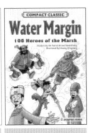

中华文化的故事

编著 ：李小香
绘画 ：傅春江
翻译 ：韩　玉

 亚太图书有限公司出版